WORKING DAZE v2.0

WORKING DAZE v2.0

MANAGERS AND OTHER UNNATURAL DISASTERS

words by **JOHN ZAKOUR**   pictures by **KYLE MILLER**

METROPOLIS INK

METROPOLIS INK
USA / Australia

web: www.metropolisink.com

email: support@metropolisink.com

This book is dedicated to all our readers
and everybody that works.

Acknowledgements

I would be amiss if I didn't acknowledge my workmates at the New York State Agricultural Experiment Station. Many of them have given me much needed inspiration either with character traits or with specific gags. I thank you all for your patience with me.

I would, of course, also like to thank my wife, Olga, and my son, Jay, just for putting up with me in general.

And of course United Media deserves thanks for making *Working Daze* available to the world.

John Z

INTRODUCTION

This book is mostly cartoons from the comic panel *Working Daze*. *Working Daze* is syndicated in a few lucky papers and over the web by United Media. We call this book an *extended* cartoon collection because it also adds a few witticisms and handy hints here and there, just to be different.

Working Daze highlights (well, mostly skews) the trials and tribulations we all go through in our daily work lives when dealing with a group of individuals and a corporate "mind set." It doesn't take place in your office, but sometimes you swear it does.

The title of this book and much of the content was inspired by managers and management everywhere. I think if you've ever been managed by anybody or managed anybody, you should certainly be able to relate to it. I don't think managers are inheritably evil, though they may often appear that way. It just happens that managers are usually more clueless and helpless than anything else.

Business, like it or not, is often governed by Murphy's Law and the Peter Principle. Murphy's Law says that pretty much *anything that can go wrong will*. To further complicate matters, those that are handling these problems won't necessarily be the best people to handle them as (per the Peter Principle) sooner or later in business almost everybody *gets promoted past their level of competence*. To make things even more interesting, many people who are managers aren't trained to be managers. Plus, even if managers are trained to manage, "management science" is about as reliable as astrology when it comes to predicting how people will react when dealing with dilemmas.

There is also a lesser known "law" that roughly states: "*The top ten percent of the people in any organization do fifty percent of the work.*" On reflection and general observation I find this statement to be strikingly accurate much more often than not. Social "sloughing" is alive and thriving in the working world.

Finally, I am a firm believer that today businesses are often governed more by profit and empire building than by putting out the best product the best way.

The cartoons in this book are a fairly accurate reflection of my slightly slanted look at today's working world. I feel that, while life may not often be fair, it can be funny, and working life can be even funnier. When life gets tough, sometimes our only defense is to sit back, relax, and laugh at it a little. That's where these cartoons come in; hopefully they will give you a little laugh or a smile—maybe even make you say to yourself, *Yep, that's how it works!*

I hope you enjoy the read.

THE CAST OF CHARACTERS

Jay, programmer, consultant, whatever. Years with the company have made him a bit cynical. Though he tries to hold his tongue he usually fails.

Carolina, web guru. She's smart and pretty, and she knows it. To top it off, she's bilingual and her second language isn't Klingon.

Roy, tech guy. An expert with machines, but clueless with people. Proud to be fluent in Klingon.

Sal, annoying customer service rep. He's not good with people *or* machines.

Ed, programmer. Expends far more energy avoiding work than working.

Andrew, graphic designer, the office cool guy. Good with people but not so good with computers.

Dana, overworked, under-appreciated, office manager. She's a mom to all—whether they like it or not. Seems to have super-human ability to get job done.

Rita, group manager. Thinks "bottom line," unless it would mean her suffering. She wants power. She *craves* power! She's just not sure what to do with it.

Sue, technical writer and office busybody. She's jealous that others have more power or are better-looking.

Jay's computer. It seems to have a mind of its own—with goals that are opposite Jay's.

9

THE CARTOONS

Most staff members tend to either over-
value or under-value their contributions.

Some managers like to create problems just to fix them. This is kind of like walking up a down escalator; they may eventually get to the top but it will be a lot harder and take a lot longer— still, it keeps them looking busy.

In the real world common sense isn't all that common. In the business world it's even less common.

It really is possible to think *too much*. This can be just as stagnating as thinking too little. Of course most managers don't really have to worry about it.

45

JOHN ZAKOUR
KYLE MILLER

Since you got a raise last year, I'm sure you're familiar with the phrase, "what goes up must come down."

You may be getting less money, but on the bright side, I can give you more work!

Well, at least you have your health. I don't think you're working hard enough.

THINGS YOU DON'T WANT TO HEAR YOUR BOSS SAY.

In the perfect world: Delegating is the art of doing less, but getting more done.

In the real world: Delegating is the art of getting other people to do the stuff you don't want to do.

JOHN ZAKOUR
KYLE MILLER

JOHN ZAKOUR
KYLE MILLER

WORKING DAZE

JOHN ZAKOUR
KYLE MILLER

Our sales and marketing staff don't understand computers, our engineers don't understand people. Our software is buggy. Yet our CEO brings in *BILLIONS*.

Yes, isn't life *GRAND?*

WORKING DAZE
JOHN ZAKOUR
KYLE MILLER
While I appreciate the effort, there really is no need for you to break your billing down by the millisecond.

JOHN ZAKOUR
KYLE MILLER

84

JOHN ZAKOUR
KYLE MILLER

JOHN ZAKOUR
KYLE MILLER

111

Machines are far more consistent than humans. So if you've narrowed down the problem to either you or your machine—it's you.

APPENDICES

Some ways to tell your boss isn't paying attention to you

— They are snoring as you talk to them.

— You notice that they mark all your email as SPAM.

— They always call you Homer.

— They always read your name tag before talking to you.

Things to do to pass the time when you're bored at work

— Count the number of days until your retirement.

— Count the number of fellow employees who are sleeping.

— Practice sleeping with your eyes open.

— See if the vending machines have been restocked.

— Check your email.

— Play Tetris with the sound off.

— Surf the web for scores, gossip and recipes.

How to relieve stress at work

— Get up and stretch every hour.

— Keep repeating to yourself,
  "It's only a job, it's only a job!"

— Take a deep breath and count to 10.

— Mentally picture yourself in a happy place.

— Don't overwork — there's always tomorrow.

— Take time off.

— Remember there are others around you
  who you can count on to help.

— Win the lottery so you can quit.

How to succeed at work

— Listen more than you talk — unless, of course, you're a manager — then just talk and talk and talk.

— Strive to complete assignments as near to on time as possible — in other words, pick far off completion dates.

— Learn to say, "No!" once in a while. You might not be as popular, but you'll be happier.

— Surround yourself with competent workers — or if you can't do that, pick real dolts so you look better.

— Come in on time — or at least before the boss does.

— Work hard — at least while the boss is watching.

— Use a lot of proactive words like "proactive." For extra credit use proactive buzzwords. For extra, extra credit use proactive buzzwords that are acronyms.

— Find something you can blackmail the boss with.

Working Daze Q & A

1. *When did you first start drawing cartoons?*

John Zakour (*the writer guy*): As far back as I can remember, and further back than I would like to say. I sold my first cartoon in 1985. I sold my first gag in 1989. I've sold way more gags (thousands) than I have cartoons (maybe a hundred).

Kyle Miller (*the cartoon guy*): Like John, I think I've always wanted to draw cartoons. I actually started drawing before I knew how to write (I'd say spell, but some folks say I still don't know how to spell). My first cartoon was sold to *Dragon Magazine* in the early '80s. Since then, I've drawn quite a few more and even sold a couple more.

2. *Who were the cartoonists who most influenced you?*

JZ: Charles Schultz, hands down, was the biggest influence. He called me once when I was in college. It was a big thrill.

KM: My parents were big fans of "Peanuts," so Schultz had a major influence in my formative years too. I was equally inspired by animators Chuck Jones and Tex Avery.

3. *How did you get your professional start?*

JZ: When I got laid off from my computer programming job, I found a book on gag writing. I sent a few syndicated people my material and they really liked it. The rest, as they say, is history!

KM: I actually started drawing caricatures at a local amusement park soon after I got out of high school. After freelancing for a while, I finally got a job at Steve Jackson Games, who decided that after buying so much of my stuff, they might as well add me to the staff.

4. *How would you describe your style?*

JZ: As for my art style, I would say very loose, (i.e., not that good).

KM: Fast and loose? My goal is to present as much visual information in as few lines as possible. It's amazing how much information the viewer can get from a single, curved line. And I want to be the one drawing that line.

5. *Where do you get your story ideas?*

JZ: I still work at my old job a few hours a week. I find staff meetings are a great way to generate ideas.

KM: I get them from John.

6. *How did you come up with your characters?*

JZ: They are all based on people I know (they know who they are).

KM: I get them from John.

7. *Which are your favorite characters in your strip and why?*

JZ: I like them all.

KM: I'm not sure. I like Dana because she's the easiest to draw and yet she still looks great. Ed is more challenging, because his hair never behaves, but I can have a lot of fun with him. Sal refuses to come out the same way no matter how often I draw him. However, his manager (Wobo the monkey) is great fun to draw.

8. *Do you create on a daily basis? Do you prefer to work in the morning or at night?*

JZ: I write Working Daze when the mood hits, usually early in the morning or late at night. It's weird. I try to have a week's worth done by Thursday.

KM: (Or when I bug him about it.) But once I get the script from John, I try to get the pencils done during the week and finish the cartoons on the weekend. I try to keep three weeks ahead of the deadline.

9. *What materials do you use to draw your comics? Do you use a computer?*

JZ: When I write, Microsoft Word. When I draw, I use a felt tip and paper then scan it.

KM: I use DerWent studio pencils for my roughs, then I use a mechanical pencil to clean them up. The finished pencils are scanned into my computer, where I add the dialog (fonts by Blambot) and ink the drawings in Adobe Illustrator using a pressure-sensitive tablet. I then add colors and shading in Adobe Photoshop.

10. *Do you have any suggestions on how to become a professional cartoonist?*

JZ: Write what you know. Keep plugging away. Listen to advice. Don't get discouraged by a rejection or two. After about 10 or 20 rejections, though, you should probably take a step back and reconsider.

KM: To be a good cartoonist, you need to be a good artist. If you don't know the basics (layout, composition, anatomy, etc.) you should learn them. The art of cartooning requires taking something well known and reducing it to a very sketchy, abbreviated form, yet still keeping it recognizable. To do that, it helps if the artist has a basic understanding of what they're trying to abbreviate. Oh, and practice, practice, practice!

About the Authors

JOHN ZAKOUR is a humor writer with a Master's degree in Human Behavior. He has written zillions (well, thousands) of gags for syndicated comics and comedians (including Marmaduke, Rugrats, Grimmy, and Dennis the Menace, and Joan Rivers' old TV show). John's humorous SF book, *The Plutonium Blonde* (DAW, 2001, co-written with Larry Ganem), was named one of the top 30 SF books of 2001 by *The Chronicle of Science Fiction*. His second novel, *The Doomsday Brunette* (DAW, Feb. 2004), has made the Locus best seller's list. John's humorous look at pregnancy, *A Man's Guide To Pregnancy*, is published by Metropolis Ink and selling well at Motherhood Maternity stores all over the country and in Canada.

John is also a regular contributor to *Nickelodeon* magazine writing Fairly Odd Parents and Jimmy Neutron stories. John has written three books on HTML (for Waite Press) and a number of children's books for a book packager. He's also sold hundreds of greeting cards to Hallmark, Recycled Paper Products, Gibson, and many others. John has sold two screenplays: "Saucer Girls" to Plutonium Films (though he's sure it won't ever get made) and the short feature "A Date with Death" that is being produced in England. John has also written and helped develop an animated series called "Prime Squad" for MUV Technologies in India. John was also a multiple-time finalist in the America's Best Screenplay contest in three different divisions.

John lives in upstate New York with his wife, Olga, a professor at Cornell University, and his son, Jay. Back in the old days (the late 1990s) John worked as science writer/web guru for Cornell University. In the 1980s John was a freelance computer game programmer. John has also been an EMT and a judo instructor. He's flexible and fast. Currently, just for fun, John is working on his Ph.D. in holistic nutrition. For fun John also enjoys the martial arts, softball, and just relaxing and watching TV.

When he's not drawing cartoons, **KYLE MILLER** makes his living as a game designer. He may be best known for his work on *Toon, The Cartoon Role-playing Game* for Steve Jackson Games. While there, he also worked on *Car Wars, GURPS, OGRE, Illuminati* and *Isaac Asimov's Star Frontiers*. Kyle was the sole designer and creative influence for the best selling *3D Ultra* pinball series for Sierra games, which includes five titles for the PC, Macintosh, and the Gameboy. In addition to drawing cartoons and making games (too many to mention here) Kyle has also held jobs at a toy store, movie theatre, and even the Johnson Space Center in Houston.

Kyle currently makes his home near Chicago, Illinois, where he lives with his wife of 18 years, his two children, and their dog (otherwise known as the fur distribution system). Kyle has heard many stories about spare time and is very interested in acquiring some for personal use.

Virtual Frustration Relievers

At times we all get frustrated with our computers. They are either too slow or just not doing what we want them to do. You want to smash them! But you can't, as smashing your computer just doesn't look good on your resume (unless of course you happen to be a garbage man).

Here's the solution! Simply cut out these virtual frustration relievers, which happen to represent your computer. You can fold, spindle and mutilate these to your heart's content.

A note to our readers

If you like *Working Daze*, write or call your local paper
and ask them to consider adding it to their comics.
Heck, even if you don't like *Working Daze* give them
a call anyhow!